Sally Ride

The First American Woman in Space

By Tom Riddolls

Crabtree Publishing Company
www.crabtreebooks.com

Crabtree Publishing Company

www.crabtreebooks.com

Author: Tom Riddolis
Publishing plan research and development:
    Sean Charlebois, Reagan Miller
    Crabtree Publishing Company
Editors: Mark Sachner, Lynn Peppas
Proofreader: Wendy Scavuzzo
Indexer: Wendy Scavuzzo
Editorial director: Kathy Middleton
Photo researcher: Ruth Owen
Designer: Alix Wood
Production coordinator: Margaret Amy Salter
Production: Kim Richardson
Prepress technician: Margaret Amy Salter

Written, developed, and produced by
Water Buffalo Books

Publisher's note:
All quotations in this book come from original sources and contain the spelling and grammatical inconsistencies of the original text. The use of such constructions is for the sake of preserving the historical and literary accuracy of the sources.

Photographs and reproductions:
Flickr (Creative Commons): page 91
NASA Images: front cover (all); page 1; page 4 (all); page 5; page 7; page 9; page 13; page 15; page 27; page 28; page 31; page 32; page 33; page 35; page 37; page 38; page 43; page 45; page 46; page 53; page 57; page 59 (all); page 61; page 63; page 65 (all); page 66; page 67; page 69; page 72; page 77 (all); page 78; page 85; page 87; page 93; page 99; page 103
Shutterstock: page 16; page 17; page 19; page 39; page 49; page 51; page 54; page 55; page 82; page 83; page 95; page 101
Spacefacts: page 41 (top)
Wikipedia (public domain): page 11; page 23; page 41 (bottom); page 75; page 80

Cover: Astronaut Sally Ride, the first American female in space, served as a mission specialist on the space shuttle *Challenger*, both in 1983 and 1984. Her job was to operate and monitor the equipment aboard the shuttle and be involved in the mission's specific tasks. Frequent monitoring of equipment was crucial to the success of the mission, as well as the crew's safety. Sally became so attached to her operations checklists, she kept them as souvenirs.

Library and Archives Canada Cataloguing in Publication

Riddolls, Tom
    Sally Ride : the first American woman in space /
Tom Riddolls.

(Crabtree groundbreaker biographies)
Includes index.
Issued also in an electronic format.
ISBN 978-0-7787-2541-1 (bound).--ISBN 978-0-7787-2550-3 (pbk.)

    1. Ride, Sally--Juvenile literature. 2. United States. National Aeronautics and Space Administration--Biography--Juvenile literature. 3. Women astronauts--United States--Biography-- Juvenile literature. 4. Astronauts--United States--Biography-- Juvenile literature. 5. Women physicists--United States-- Biography--Juvenile literature. I. Title. II. Series: Crabtree groundbreaker biographies

TL789.85.R53R53 2011   j629.450092   C2010-903038-9

Library of Congress Cataloging-in-Publication Data

Riddolls, Tom.
    Sally Ride : the first American woman in space /
Tom Riddolls.
        p. cm. -- (Crabtree groundbreaker biographies)
    Includes index.
    ISBN 978-0-7787-2550-3 (pbk. : alk. paper) --
    ISBN 978-0-7787-2541-1 (reinforced library binding : alk. paper) -- ISBN 978-1-4271-9473-2 (electronic (PDF))
    1. Ride, Sally--Juvenile literature. 2. Women astronauts-- United States--Biography--Juvenile literature. 3. Astronauts-- United States--Biography--Juvenile literature. 4. United States. National Aeronautics and Space Administration-- Biography--Juvenile literature. 5. Women physicists--United States--Biography--Juvenile literature. I. Title. II. Series.

    TL789.85.R53R53 2011
    629.450092--dc22
    [B]
                                                                    2010018113

Crabtree Publishing Company

www.crabtreebooks.com   1-800-387-7650

Printed in the USA/082010/BL20100723

Published in Canada
Crabtree Publishing
616 Welland Ave.
St. Catharines, Ontario
L2M 5V6

Published in the United States
Crabtree Publishing
PMB 59051
350 Fifth Avenue, 59th Floor
New York, New York 10118

Published in the United Kingdom
Crabtree Publishing
Maritime House
Basin Road North, Hove
BN41 1WR

Published in Australia
Crabtree Publishing
386 Mt. Alexander Rd.
Ascot Vale (Melbourne)
VIC 3032

Contents

Chapter 1
The First Up There

The shuttle rattled and shook, and the intense roar of the engines echoed deep in Sally's stomach. Sally says that when the shuttle begins to shift at liftoff "there's no more time to wonder, and no time to be scared." Eight and a half minutes later, there was suddenly silence as the shuttle's engines were shut down and the void of space enveloped the shuttle.

Liftoff

The day was June 18, 1983, and Sally had become the first American female in space. "She is flying with us because she is the very best person for the job. There is no man I would rather have in her place," said Robert Crippen, Sally's flight commander.

Sally's big day began at 2:30 a.m., in a hotel not far from Cape Canaveral, when she and her crewmates awoke. The final week of training

Opposite: A dramatic view of the Remote Manipulator System (RMS), a robotic arm that Sally Ride helped develop with NASA and trained extensively to use on her missions aboard the space shuttle.

had been somewhat uneventful. There were no big send-off parties, no good luck pats on the shoulders from instructors, friends, or family. This was because the crew had been cut off from human contact to ensure they were not exposed to an illness that could ruin the mission.

A couple of hours later, the five crew members walked into the shuttle. The site was curiously quiet, with only the hum of equipment breaking the silence. It was only 4:45 a.m., and the ground below and the sea to the east were lost in the darkness. With bulky helmets and gloves on, the crew members were strapped into their seats.Then the wait began.

The seconds, minutes, and hours ticked by as Mission Control prepared for launch. The crew, on the other hand, had very little to do. With their feet up in the air and their faces flush with blood, the astronauts made small talk and responded to the few questions and instructions from Mission Control.

At T minus six seconds, the main engines on the shuttle burst into life, filling the crew cabin with a dull roar. The shuttle tilted on the platform, and its nose began to lurch forward. The shuttle was still bolted to the platform, and the entire vehicle was straining against the pressure from the three main engines.

T minus five seconds: Main engines were at 90 percent full power, all systems good.

T minus four seconds: The nose continued to angle forward another foot (30 cm). The pressure readings from inside the fuel tanks looked good.

Challenger *clears the launch pad at the start of Mission STS–7 on June 18, 1983, with Sally Ride and four other crew members aboard.*

1983

The year 1983 was one of development and change, not just for the space program. IBM had released the first desktop computer with a hard drive as standard equipment; the first African-American was elected Miss America; and Madonna's first album hit the stores.

T minus three seconds: The engines were now at 100 percent power.

T minus two seconds: flames from the exhaust shot beneath the launch pad at the speed of sound.

One second to liftoff: the shuttle sprang back to a completely vertical position. Astronauts called this "twang."

T minus zero: the bolts holding the shuttle in place were released at the same moment that the solid rocket boosters ignited. Suddenly, things got a lot noisier and the shaking got much worse.

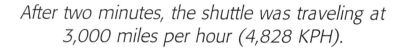

After two minutes, the shuttle was traveling at 3,000 miles per hour (4,828 KPH).

Within moments, the shuttle was traveling at over 100 miles (161 km) per hour. At this point, the computer was flying the shuttle, and Sally and the rest of the crew were just there for the ride. Any adjustments made to the position of the shuttle while under such thrust were too small for humans to attempt.

After two minutes, the shuttle was traveling at 3,000 miles per hour (4,828 KPH). The shuttle was almost 30 miles (48 km) above the Atlantic. Small explosions were felt as the bolts that held the solid rocket boosters to the external fuel tank exploded and the rockets flew off to the sides.

After another six minutes, the members of the crew were still being pressed back into their seats as the main engines continued to burn. The thin atmosphere meant less friction, however, and therefore a much smoother ride. The shuttle was now flying almost level to Earth's surface but 150 miles (241 km) up. In the next minute, the effects of gravity rapidly decreased, and the shuttle accelerated into the emptiness of space. The roar of the engines was now a silent vibration.

"All adventures, especially into new territory, are scary."

Sally Ride

Astronauts of the STS–7/Challenger mission are, from left to right, first row: Sally K. Ride (mission specialist), Robert L. Crippen (commander), and Frederick H. Hauck (pilot); rear row: John M. Fabian (left) and Norman E. Thagard, (mission specialists).

At last, at T plus eight minutes 30 seconds, the main engines were cut off and the crew members were suddenly weightless. Despite the peaceful calm that descended on the cabin, the crew was actually hurtling through space at 18,000 miles per hour (28,968 KPH). The crew members allowed themselves some cheering and slaps on the shoulders as they unbuckled their belts. The celebration did not last long. There was a lot of work to be done in the next six days.

THE SPACE SHUTTLE

The space shuttle spacecraft were built to replace the Apollo program, which put humans on the Moon in 1969. Five different shuttles were built, each similar to the others. Unlike previous spacecraft, each shuttle was to be largely reusable. The shuttle also differed from previous craft because it could carry large amounts of equipment and as many as eight passengers.

NASA calls each of its shuttles "the most complex machine ever built"—and it just might be. It has over 2.5 million parts, 230 miles (370 km) of wire, more than 1,060 plumbing valves and connections, over 1,440 circuit breakers, and over 27,000 insulating tiles that protect it from extreme temperatures. On a mission, the shuttle will experience temperatures that range from -250 °F (-157 °C) in space to as high as 3,000 °F (1,650 °C) as it re-enters the atmosphere. The biggest cost of the missions is the fuel. Just before launch, the shuttle weighs 4.5 million pounds (2.0 million kilograms), but most of that is fuel. Eight minutes after launch, the shuttle only weighs 1.0 million pounds (0.5 million kg).

With the space shuttle's retirement following its 2010 launches, it is not yet clear what spacecraft will replace it.

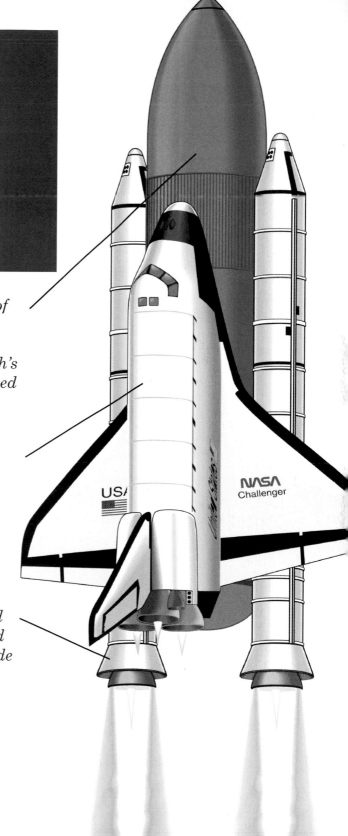

> *"When you're getting ready to launch into space, you're sitting on a big explosion waiting to happen. "*
>
> Sally Ride,
> describing liftoff

External Fuel Tank: *This part of the shuttle is not used more than once. It contains the fuel that gets the shuttle into space. Out of Earth's atmosphere, the fuel tank is released and falls away from the shuttle.*

Orbiter: *This is the part of the shuttle where the crew lives and works. It is the only part of the shuttle that re-enters Earth's atmosphere, lands, and is made ready for another journey.*

Solid Rocket Boosters: *The solid rocket boosters are filled with solid fuel, like a firecracker. They provide power during liftoff. They are released from the shuttle at about two minutes after liftoff. They are recovered and reused.*

Chapter 2
Before the Stars

Sally Ride is an exceptional woman with an unexceptional beginning. As a student, Sally was considered clever, but not extraordinary. What she did do as a teenager—what she has always done—was set her goals on things that appealed to her. Success did not follow her everywhere, but she always explored her options. In the end, it was this openness to trying new things that led her to the stars.

Tennis or Science?

In the summer of 1951, Walt Disney's cartoon *Alice in Wonderland* was doing well in the box office. With World War II several years behind them, most Americans were ready to look to the future. In Encino, a suburb of Los Angeles, California, Carol Joyce and Dale Burdell Ride had their first child—an ordinary American

She was a big sports fan, and she was smart. By age five, she was reading the sports page of the newspaper.

girl who would forge a path into the unknown. Her name was Sally Kristen Ride.

Sally's first decade was that of the average middle-class American child. She and her younger sister Karen enjoyed being active and being outdoors. She was a big sports fan, and she was smart. By age five, she was reading the sports page of the newspaper. She became a huge baseball fan and even said she wished she could play shortstop for the Dodgers, who had moved to LA from Brooklyn, New York, in 1958. Karen recalls of her big sister:

"When the kids played baseball or football out in the streets, Sally was always the best. When they chose up sides, Sally was always the first to be chosen. She was the only girl who was acceptable to the boys."

Sally's parents were very involved in the Presbyterian Church. Her mom was a counselor at the County Jail, and her dad worked at Santa Monica College. Of them, Sally says:

"My parents must have done a great job. Anytime I wanted to pursue something that they weren't familiar with, that was not part of their lifestyle, they let me go ahead and do it. Tennis was an example; so was going into science. I think they were kind of glad when I went into the astronaut program, because that was something they could understand. Astrophysics they had trouble with."

Sally's mother puts the parenting Sally and her sister received this way: "In a way you

Several of NASA's first female candidates take a break from training in Florida in 1978. From left: Sally Ride, Judy Resnik, Anna Fisher, Kathryn Sullivan, and Rhea Seddon. Resnik was one of the seven crew members killed in the Challenger *disaster in 1986.*

could look at it as neglect," she laughs. "Dale and I simply forgot to tell them that there were things they couldn't do. But I think if it had occurred to us to tell them, we would have refrained." She said that she taught her daughters to excel, not to conform. Sally's mother seemed to also have a quirky side, something her famous daughter is famous for, too. When Sally and Karen wanted a dog, their mother only relented and let them get a collie after she had recarpeted the house in collie colors so that dog hairs would not show!

At school, Sally was a good student, but shy. She said,

"I liked some classes, I didn't like others. I looked forward to getting out of school every day, and getting onto the playground or getting home to play with my friends, but I didn't really mind going to school as much as some of my classmates did and as much as a lot of kids do."

She found history and English difficult, while science and math came easily. She was quiet and didn't really like being called upon to answer questions or speak to the class: "I think that my most stressful moments were probably sitting in class, huddled down, hoping that the teacher didn't notice me and call on me. Whether I knew the answer or not, that was irrelevant."

Sally also remembered something else about her school days—when the teacher wheeled a big black-and-white television into the classroom so the students could watch the launch of an early space capsule. She thought a lot about what it would be like to be in space.

Sally read a lot as a child, including classic children's science fiction like the *Danny Dunn* books, and all the *Nancy Drew* mysteries. She also read comic books, *Mad* magazine, and *Scientific American*, which her parents subscribed to because of Sally's interest in science.

In 1961, Sally's father took a year off and took the family to Europe. It taught her that changing one's direction in life was not only acceptable, but it exposed one to new ways of thinking and living. This ability to pick up and change directions was a trait that stayed with Sally into her adult years.

It was when the family was in Spain that Sally discovered she had a knack for tennis. She practiced as much as she could, and after the family returned to the States a year later, Sally won a scholarship to Westlake School for Girls, a famous and expensive private school near her home in Encino.

This scholarship was very important to Sally in two ways. First, as a natural athlete, she had hopes of becoming a professional tennis player, and Westlake encouraged and promoted its student athletes. Second, Westlake was a very good academic school, and the scholarship gave Sally the opportunity to receive an excellent education.

"I was a pretty good kid. I had my moments, but I was a pretty good kid."

Sally Ride

Sally was an outstanding athlete. Once, in science class, she participated in an experiment to demonstrate the difference between the pulse rate before and after exercise. Sally ran around the whole campus, but it hardly affected her pulse rate at all! For years at school, Sally worked on her tennis skills and, by the time she graduated from Westlake in 1968, she was the captain of her tennis team. She was also ranked 18th on the national junior tennis circuit, the semi-professional league of players under the age of 18.

After graduating from high school, Sally enrolled in Swarthmore College in Pennsylvania. While many Swarthmore students are active athletes, Sally was more dedicated to her game than most. About a year and a half after entering Swarthmore, she decided, "What was I thinking? I should have been a professional tennis player." She dropped out of college so she could train in tennis full-time. The decision did not go over well with her parents, but she moved back to Southern California and focused on tennis. Sally explains:

"I had this very, very strong feeling that I had something in me that I hadn't really explored, and it was, 'How good a tennis player could I be? Could I be good enough to be a professional tennis player? There is no way I am going to find this out at Swarthmore College, and if I wait until after I graduate, it will likely be too late.'"

This time away from school proved to be a testing ground for Sally. She said, "I took a long, hard look at my forehand and realized that I was not going to make a fortune with that forehand." At the end of three months, she knew that she did not have what it took to become a professional tennis player, even though she was very good. She quit tennis and went back to college, at Stanford University, which was close to home. Here, as well as being on the tennis team, she could reacquaint herself with one of her other interests: science. Remembering her early years at Westlake, Sally said, "I had planned on a career in science from high school on."

> *"I knew that for me, science was a better long-term career than tennis."*
>
> Sally Ride,
> on quitting tennis

Sally's Physics

With a new focus on science as a career, Sally enrolled in the physics program of Stanford University. It was 1968. Over the next ten years, she earned a Bachelor's Degree in science and a Bachelor's Degree in English Literature, both at Stanford. Even though she explored English at the university level, there was never any question about the field of study in which her main interests lay. Sally said, "I majored in physics almost from the first day I walked into college and continued on as a physics major in college and then in graduate school." She said that she took English courses to get some balance into her life. Initially, she took them "pretty much on a whim" because she had a friend who was an English major. After trying some courses, she found she really liked them, particularly Shakespearean literature. By the time she'd graduated, she'd taken enough English courses to major in the subject.

Sally was an excellent student at Stanford. Her college roommate, Molly Tyson, remembers that Sally "wasn't one of those people who had to study all the time.... She's a problem solver who approached courses by saying, 'Here's an interesting problem. Let's get to the bottom of it.'" Molly said she had "never seen Sally trip, on or off the court, physically or intellectually." She saw Sally as a normal young person who would "go into and out of health food phases" and "into and out of Big Mac phases."

Sally continued with physics and, after completing her Master's Degree in science in 1973, she stayed in school, doing doctoral work and earning her Ph.D. in physics in 1977. Both of her graduate degrees, like her undergraduate degree, were from Stanford.

In her last year at Stanford she saw an advertisement in the university newsletter that would change the direction of her life once again. "All that time I had a real interest in astronomy, astrophysics, and the space program," Sally said. It is no wonder that she responded to the job ad. It was from NASA, and they were looking for astronauts. Sally knew immediately she wanted to do it. "It's something that was just deep inside me," she said. "There is really no other way to describe it."

> *"I'm so excited. I'd like to go up tomorrow!"*
>
> Sally Ride, on being selected as an astronaut

Wanted: Astronauts

The want ad NASA published across the United States in July 1977 was the first call for astronauts in over ten years. The response from the public was strong. Over 8,000 applicants were interested, though there were only 35 spots in the training program. Sally was delighted to be accepted.

NASA does not select its astronauts from a specific group of people. Rather, astronauts are selected from the general public and from all walks of life. Sally Ride had not gone to school to be an astronaut. Instead, she was a scientist with an interest in space. Before she saw the advertisement in her university newsletter, she had not considered the job. "I followed the space program, as a lot of people did," Sally explained. "… [A]s soon as I saw the ad I knew I wanted to apply."

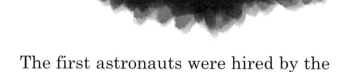

Astronauts also have to be very fit, intelligent, and calm. They must also be excellent problem solvers.

The first astronauts were hired by the United States back in 1959, before the nation had any experience with space flight. These very first astronauts were selected from the military. It was a good idea then to hire people who were skilled at flying experimental aircraft, and the best pilots most often flew in the U.S. Air Force. Of the 500 men who were interviewed in the 1950s, NASA selected seven pilots as the nation's first astronauts. They were all from the air force.

By 1977, when Sally applied for the astronaut job, times had changed, and women were finally being admitted to the program. In fact, "by the time that NASA got around to selecting our group of astronauts, they had

A CENTURY OF SEARCHING

The National Aeronautics and Space Administration, or NASA, had its beginnings with a scientist named Charles Walcott, who worked at the Smithsonian Museum investigating fossil insects. Walcott was involved in an effort to create a committee to investigate the relatively new field of aeronautics.

In 1915, he helped get a law through Congress creating NACA, the National Advisory Committee for Aeronautics. By 1958, the "space race" between the United States and the Soviet Union had helped make the exploration of outer space a new national priority. It was time to expand the mission of NACA to include these new aspirations and, that year, the committee was essentially dissolved and reborn as today's National Aeronautics and Space Administration, known to all as NASA. NASA's stated mission: "To improve life here; To extend life to there; To find life beyond."

The NASA logo outside the Kennedy Space Center in Florida

made it very clear a couple years before that this group was going to include women," she said.

Though Sally's background included athletics and a Ph.D. in physics, neither of these attributes were necessary job requirements. In fact, many famous athletes would not make good astronauts because they are too big. Spacecraft are not very big inside, so there is a height restriction. No astronauts are taller than 5 feet 11 inches (1.8 m). Many athletes are taller than that. Astronauts also have to be very fit, intelligent, and calm. They must also be excellent problem solvers. Sally's background as an athlete and a scientist, while not part of the job description, helped her develop qualities such as these. Sally said that "One thing I probably share with everyone else in the astronaut office is composure." About what it takes to be an astronaut, she said, "We're really all very similar. We're all people who are dedicated to the space program and who really want to fly in the space shuttle. That's a common characteristic that we all have that transcends the different backgrounds."

The New Recruits

Sally and her fellow new recruits moved to the Johnson Space Center in Houston, Texas, where they entered training. Sally said it was tough for everyone, but tougher for the women. Having six women gave them a little security in numbers. Also, the male astronauts they were working with were accustomed to working with women. Nonetheless, as Sally explained, NASA was very male dominated:

"Out of roughly 4,000 technical employees at the Johnson Space Center—4,000 or so scientists and engineers—I think there were only four women, so that gives you a sense of how male the culture was. When we arrived, we more than doubled the number of women with Ph.D.s at the center."

Sally and her 34 fellow new trainees spent much of their first year learning about the space shuttle. They were to be the first group to get to use it. This learning was done mostly in the classroom. The astronauts' teachers were the engineers and scientists who helped build and design the spacecraft. Sally and her classmates got to ask detailed questions about how the shuttle worked from the only people in the world that knew the answers. Even with a host of people working behind the scenes back on Earth, astronauts are still relatively isolated when they are in their spacecraft, and they have to understand how the shuttle works so they can fix it when something breaks.

Besides having to know the shuttle and how it works, the astronauts would have to play the role of each other's doctors in space, and so they also learned basic health care. For the same reason, they needed to learn basic dental care. What's more, the astronauts had to understand the jobs of their fellow crew members. If someone became ill while in orbit, the others would need to be able to take his or her place. There were cameras to learn to operate, launch protocol to understand, and the physics of flying in Earth's orbit to master.

Space Training

Sally's class of astronauts was broken up, and each person was assigned to a smaller group that would form a mission crew. Of the 35 new astronauts, Sally was chosen for the crew that would go up into space on the seventh space shuttle flight. This was a very big deal. As Sally describes it, her reaction was, "'Oh my gosh, I can't believe that I get a chance to do this.' And it was only after that, not long after that, but after that, that I thought, 'Oh my gosh, I am going to be the first woman to get to go up, representing this country.'"

Since every mission is different, a crew is picked based on their skills and knowledge to ensure the mission's tasks are well matched with the employees chosen to perform them. Sally's mission was called STS–7. The letters STS stand for Space Transport System, otherwise known as the space shuttle. There were four other astronauts assigned to STS–7 with her.

Sally's knowledge of astrophysics and her keen sense of balance and movement— perfected over a decade earlier on the tennis court—helped make her ideal for operating equipment. Her mission involved using the robotic arm to launch and retrieve satellites for the first time. Launching a multi-million dollar satellite is not easy. Satellites must be placed in orbit at just the right angle and in a way that ensures they do not spin or fly off in the wrong direction. If a satellite does spin or fly away, it will not operate correctly, and all the money spent to build it will be wasted. Sally had helped design the robotic arm

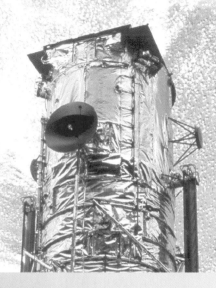

Astronaut F. Story Musgrave is anchored on the end of the Remote Manipulator System (RMS) arm, ready to work on the Hubble Space Telescope. Astronaut Jeffrey A. Hoffman is inside the payload bay. He will assist Musgrave.

THE REMOTE MANIPULATOR SYSTEM

The robotic arm Sally helped develop with NASA was called the Remote Manipulator System (RMS). The RMS was 50 feet (15 m) long and designed to do a variety of tasks in space. An important job was to take a satellite brought into space by the shuttle and place it in orbit, or to pick a satellite out of orbit and put it into the shuttle to be brought back to Earth. The RMS was also used to perform tasks such as filming space walks and inspecting the outside of the shuttle for damage. Sally spent hundreds of hours training to use the RMS.

A suit technician helps Sally strap herself into a seat in the shuttle mission simulator in Houston on May 23, 1983, less than a month before her first launch.

during her first year of training, and was very good at operating it. Clearly, she was the right person for this job. As the leader of the mission, commander Robert Crippen explained, "I wanted people who knew the arm well ... Sally and John [Fabian] were experts. I wanted a competent engineer who was cool under stress. Sally had demonstrated that talent. Sally also has a pleasing personality that will fit in with the group."

Together, the crew of STS–7 practiced how to launch satellites and repair fuel leaks. They practiced everything— even using the toilet. They memorized the stars and their positions in the sky and learned how to fly a jet plane. No questions were left unasked.

In all of the months leading up to a mission, the most important training the crew members received was inside simulators. They practiced take-offs and landings over and over in a model of the real shuttle. This repeated practice was important because the shuttle and its crew are at the most risk during the entry into orbit and the re-entry into Earth's atmosphere. When floating high above Earth, the shuttle is at rest and not as much can go wrong. When rocketing upward at thousands of miles per hour, however, a very minor problem can quickly lead to disaster. It was in the simulator that Sally and her group learned to work as a team. This teamwork could potentially save their lives later on in the mission.

All the work and tasks anticipated during a mission are rehearsed. To get astronauts accustomed to the feeling of weightlessness, they are taken on an airplane that the astronauts have nicknamed "the vomit comet." The vomit comet flies up and down, in a pattern similar to that of a roller coaster. As the plane reaches the top of an arc, it angles with its nose down until it reaches the bottom of the arc. During this downward flight, passengers float freely and can move about the cabin just as if they were in space. The weightlessness lasts about half a minute.

Sally flew on the vomit comet many times

"... [T]hen once you have learned it all, you have to practice, practice, practice, practice, practice, practice, practice until everything is second nature."

Sally Ride, on the rigors of training

and did thousands of freefalls. At that time, NASA was using a KC–135 aircraft. Many different planes have been used for these flights, but the KC–135 is the largest.

It has enough room inside for astronauts to experience weightlessness while dressed in a space suit. While the vomit comet gives trainees some idea of what it will feel like in space without Earth's gravity, it does not last long enough for anyone to find out whether an astronaut will suffer from severe nausea and illness when they are in space.

When asked to describe astronaut training, Sally has said that it was very difficult—more for its mental training than physical training. The need to learn all there was to know about the space shuttle, plus preparing for anything that could possibly go wrong, was more difficult than most people might imagine. Along with the need to practice, this training took years.

Despite the challenges, Sally characteristically took it all in stride. She was confident that space travel was exactly what she wanted to be doing, and that she could do it.

> *"I knew how to study, I knew how to concentrate and to dedicate myself to learning one particular area, and that's what I was doing again, so I was fairly confident and comfortable actually in the environment."*
>
> Sally Ride

Flight commander John W. Young (left) and pilot Robert L. Crippen, the prime crew members for NASA's first space shuttle flight, Mission STS–1, are shown logging time in the shuttle orbiter Columbia *during a training session at the Kennedy Space Center in October 1980.*

THE SHUTTLE SIMULATOR

The shuttle simulator is a large metal box on moveable legs on the outside and an exact replica of the space shuttle on the inside. During training periods, a crew would learn the sequence of the hundreds of tasks required during liftoff and re-entry. Once they mastered the basics, the instructors would create "problems" for the crew. These might mean simulating a leaking fuel tank or an electrical blackout, or both. The crew members then must find out what went wrong and correct it, all while safely flying the shuttle. These simulations might have lasted a matter of minutes or hours. For the longer simulations, the crew had their space food meals in the fake shuttle."

On September 6, 1984, crew members enjoy a "light" moment in space aboard the shuttle Discovery. *They are (counter-clockwise from center) crew commander Henry W. Hartsfield Jr., pilot Michael L. Coats, mission specialists Steven A. Hawley and Judith A. Resnik, payload specialist Charles D. Walker, and mission specialist Richard M. Mullane. Hawley and Sally Ride were married in 1982.*

She felt that her many years as a student–from high school through college–and her work on her Ph.D., had given her the ability to learn things.

During the same period that Sally Ride was training, she was dating a fellow astronaut, Steve Hawley. The pair was married in 1982, at the groom's family home in Kansas. Sally flew her own plane to the ceremony. Steve was also an astronaut in training, and the couple lived in the suburbs near the space center where they worked. They were very private, avoided appearing in public together, and did not allow media staff into their home. Steve flew into space 13 months after Sally. They never did get to fly together. NASA does not assign married couples to the same missions.

In all, Sally spent five years training to become an astronaut before she climbed into the space shuttle, ready to launch.

BEING "HOUSTON"

In 1969, when Neil Armstrong landed the *Eagle* spacecraft on the Moon, he said these words: "Houston, Tranquility Base here. The *Eagle* has landed." Who was this "Houston" he was talking to? Was he addressing the people of Houston, Texas? No, he was speaking with Charles Duke, an astronaut in training and the CAPCOM for the *Apollo 11* mission. CAPCOM stands for Capsule Commander. This person's job is to communicate with astronauts in space. At any one time, there is only one person communicating with the astronauts in space. All information exchanged between Earth and people in space goes through a CAPCOM.

Astronauts understand each other and use the same words to describe the complicated business of flying spacecraft. "Houston" is the call sign used for the CAPCOM. A call sign is the name used on the radio. It is a unique identifier that is easily heard and recognized. Anyone who is listening and hears a call sign knows who is being addressed. Whenever astronauts talk to "Houston," they are talking to the CAPCOM on duty. Sally had the important position of CAPCOM for two other missions, STS–2 in 1981 and STS–3 in 1982. Sally said that being CAPCOM is "an indication that people think you are doing well." She said of the job that "it really does give you that experience and kind of that inside look at Mission Control and that inside look at how another crew—the crew in orbit—works and communicates with each other."

President Ronald Reagan with NASA officials in Mission Control, Houston. He is on a long-distance call to astronauts Joe Engle and Richard Truly of the STS–2 crew while they're in space.

Chapter 3
Women in Space

The announcement that Sally Ride would be flying into space with STS–7 was met by the press with fascination, because she was a woman. She had to field many questions, such as, "Will the flight affect your reproductive organs?" and "Do you weep when things go wrong on the job?" Sally handled these queries calmly and sharply. When asked, "Will you become a mother?" she first avoided answering, then smiled and said, "You notice I'm not answering."

A Media Sensation, of Sorts

Even Johnny Carson on *The Tonight Show* joked that the shuttle launch was being postponed until Sally Ride could find the purse to match her shoes. Prior to her space flight, Sally had many thoughts about the media and their strong reaction to her gender, and she felt that "It may be too bad that our society isn't further along and that this is such a big deal."

Despite having to deal with the press occasionally, Sally's space preparations kept her pretty focused. She was simply too busy to watch the news and read newspapers, and the people around her—her crewmates and NASA staff—treated her no differently because she was a woman. "I think women ought to be able to do whatever they want to do," said crewmate

John Fabian. Sally said to the media when asked how she felt about the momentous milestone of being the first American woman in space, "I honestly don't have time to think about it."

While Sally's selection as an astronaut did much to help NASA overcome the idea that only men could be astronauts, she was not the first woman to be launched into space. That honor went to a Soviet cosmonaut, Valentina Tereshkova. Neither was Sally the first American woman to set her sights on space travel. In the United States in 1960, women did not fly spacecraft. In fact, most did not have careers. This was the age of the housewife but, one American woman, Jerrie Cobb, never quite fit this typical pattern. She never became an astronaut although she did make her mark on the early days of the space program.

Jerrie Cobb: Born Too Soon?

In the late 1950s, when NASA initially started interviewing and testing people to be astronauts, Jerrie Cobb was a young pilot. Not yet 30 years old, she had broken the speed record, the distance record and, ironically, the highest flight record—twice. Despite her tremendous skills, she was rarely taken seriously as a flier. While men wore flying suits, the few women pilots of Jerrie's day were

"It was important for women to go into space, but I wasn't a pioneer. Maybe a role model."

Sally Ride

Jerrie Cobb undergoes testing in the Multiple Axis Space Test Inertia Facility. As the machine she is strapped into spins out of control, Jerrie attempts to use the pilot controls to keep the machine "flying." Jerrie passed all the tests, but she was not allowed to become an astronaut. Only military test pilots could become astronauts and, at the time, no military test pilots were women.

Pilot Jerrie Cobb poses next to a capsule that was part of the Mercury program, the first to send an American astronaut into space. Despite their proven skills and their support of a member of the NASA selection team, Jerrie and a number of other qualified women were never allowed to enter the NASA training program.

expected to wear dresses and high heel shoes—in a jet plane! Jerrie outwitted them by changing into more appropriate flying gear in the cramped cockpit of her plane while in the air.

In the first astronaut interviews and tests, women were excluded. But one physician on the NASA team, Dr. Randy Lovelace, was worried that men were too large and could not cope with the physical stresses of space flight. Women, he thought, being smaller and more tolerant of pain and discomfort, might be more suitable. With private funding, Dr. Lovelace began putting Jerrie through the same tests as the men. After several months, Jerrie had passed every test they gave her, often better than her male counterparts.

Jerrie did so well, she and Dr. Lovelace found 12 other women to put through the same tests. One test was a machine that simulated a plane in a completely uncontrolled spin, twisting and turning faster than the eye could track. In this dizzying environment, the trainees were expected to retain control of the joystick and respond to commands. For another year, the hopeful female astronaut trainees continued to pass tests. It looked as if history would be made and they would be admitted into the space program. Then NASA simply said no; they had seven men and they did not need any more astronauts. Jerrie went to Washington and before the Space Committee said, "We ask as citizens of this nation to be allowed to participate with seriousness and sincerity in the making of history now."

John Glenn, the first American to orbit Earth in 1962, and a national hero, stood up in front of the committee and killed the dreams of Jerrie with these words:

> *"It is just a fact. The men go off and*
> *fight the wars and fly the airplanes*
> *and come back and help design*
> *and build and test them.*
> *The fact that women are not in this*
> *field is a fact of our social order."*

It would be 21 years before Sally Ride changed that social order. Jerrie and many of the other female astronaut trainees from the 1950s were there to watch the shuttle that launched Sally into history.

THE FIRST WOMAN IN SPACE

Valentina Tereshkova was born in 1937 in a small town in western Russia. Growing up, Valentina worked as a child laborer. She did not even go to school until she was ten years old, but she proved to be a bright and dedicated student. After the equivalent of high school, she got a job at a thread-making factory, and then she did something that would one day change her life. She joined a parachuting club. Valentina quickly took to her new hobby and, by the time she was 20, she had 100 jumps under her belt. In 1961, she read that the Soviet government was hoping to send a woman into space. It was her parachuting experience that made her application stand out and helped her be selected for training along with four other applicants. Valentina was no doubt the underdog, but she worked very hard during her training and she was selected for the mission. Her trip in 1963 lasted three days as she circled Earth, by herself, in a capsule that was too small to stand up in. After discovering and fixing technical difficulties that had her drifting the wrong way in orbit, Valentina got her vessel headed safely toward Earth. At about 10,000 feet (3,048 m) above the countryside of Kazakhstan, she parachuted out. Since then, Valentina became involved in politics and has become a spokesperson for women's rights.

"*Everyone should do what he or she is good at. They should do what they love. I always did what I loved—in the space program and in my present work.*"

Valentina Tereshkova, the first woman in space

Above: This photo of pioneering Soviet cosmonaut Valentina Tereshkova was taken at the time of her three-day orbital flight in 1963.

Right: a Soviet postage stamp honoring Tereshkova

Chapter 4
Living and Working in Space

Even with all the technology that we have poured into making living and working in space as safe and comfortable as possible, the fact is that space is simply not a habitable place. There is no warmth, no air to breath, and no gravity to keep supper sitting on its plate. Much of what we have come to expect from life on Earth simply does not exist in space.

Living in Space

Gravity has a huge impact on daily life. The force of gravity allows us to drink our orange juice out of glasses and keeps our dinner on its plate. Consider what it would be like if there was no "up" or "down." Our cars would be useless, as their weight is what creates the friction between the wheels and the road,

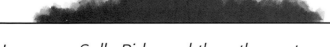

In space, Sally Ride and the other astronauts found ways to live without "up" and "down."

causing the cars to move forward. Without gravity, the tires would just spin. All the water in the rivers, lakes, and oceans would simply drift away. Without gravity, Earth would be a very untidy and unpleasant place.

In space, Sally Ride and the other astronauts found ways to live without "up" and "down." For one thing, they kept everything tucked away in cupboards. They had boxes instead of shelves, and they had Velcro sewn onto their clothes so they could stick things to themselves—and stick themselves to their seats at their workstations. Some astronauts slept in bags attached to a wall, and others slept in a compartment that was similar to a locker. Sally slept in a bag strapped to the wall.

A lot of their food was a thick paste, like mashed potatoes, so that the bits didn't float away. They drank out of pouches with straws, not glasses. During training, the astronauts had taste-tested food and decided what it was best to bring to eat while in space. Sally and her crewmates had about 75 items to choose from the NASA menu, plus 20 beverages. Food was stored and cooked in a space kitchen, a small galley with a hot and cold water dispenser, a storage locker, an oven to warm food, serving trays, and a hygiene station.

Getting Sick in Space

In space, almost half of all astronauts feel very ill when they first arrive. The illness is called space adaptation syndrome. It is not very dangerous and usually lasts only a few days. The illness is caused by confusion in the brain's system of detecting the body's position as a

On Challenger's *middeck, Sally Ride, wearing flight coveralls and a communications headset, floats alongside the middeck airlock hatch.*

result of suddenly experiencing little gravity.

NASA has found there is no way to test if someone will get space adaptation syndrome. The planning for Sally's mission to space assumed that no difficult tasks would be completed during the first two days. This is the normal way a mission is planned, just in case the astronaut assigned to the task is not feeling well. Unfortunately, for those astronauts who do suffer from space adaptation syndrome, there is nothing that can be done except wait for the ill feelings to go away. The medications that might make astronauts feel better are not used because they might make them drowsy and forgetful. Sally Ride was one of the lucky ones. She did not experience nausea and could get to work right away.

Working in Space

In a 2004 interview, Sally explained what it feels like to be at work in space:

"There's a huge amount of pressure on every astronaut, because when you get right down to it, the experiments that are conducted on a space flight, or the satellites that are carried up, the work that's to be done, is important and expensive work, and you are up there for a week or two on a space shuttle flight."

Sally went on to talk about the enormous amount of money invested in the astronauts' training and in the shuttle and all the equipment that is in it, and the kind of pressure this creates for those who are doing the experiments and other work on board the

WHO DOES WHAT IN SPACE?

On STS–7 there were five astronauts: one flight commander, one pilot, and three mission specialists. On Sally's second mission to space, there were seven astronauts, two of whom were payload specialists. Each kind of astronaut has a different role.

Commander: The commander is the boss of the shuttle. The commander has the last say in important decisions and also works with NASA ground crews to plan the mission before the launch. Everything that goes on board the shuttle, from satellites to astronauts to new toilets, must get the approval of the commander.

Pilot: The pilot's main job is to fly the shuttle. Because the shuttle is such a complicated craft, only the pilot handles the controls while the rest of the crew relay information to him.

Mission Specialist: Mission specialists are astronauts who run the shuttle. They operate the equipment, manage the schedules, and do everything else the commander and pilot do not. Mission specialists are also involved in the mission's specific tasks, such as delivering or repairing satellites or performing experiments. Sally Ride was a mission specialist.

Payload Specialist: NASA also trains some non-NASA employees to go to space as payload specialists. Usually these are scientists, sometimes from other countries, but there have also been schoolteachers. The payload specialist's job in space is to perform experiments, work with satellites, or assist the other astronauts when they need it.

craft. Added to this is the fact that "You can't make a mistake, that week or two that you're in space." The scope of errors that are possible on a mission is enormous. They range from mistakes "that would ruin some scientist on earth's experiment—career, potentially"—to damaging a satellite that a nation depends on for its communications system, to making a mistake that could cost the mission or even the lives of its crew.

An Armload of Satellites

One of Sally's main jobs on Mission STS–7 was to launch two satellites, one for the government of Indonesia, the other for a private communications company in Canada. Each satellite owner paid NASA $11 million for its satellite launch. Sally released these two satellites during the first two days of the mission, using the Remote Manipulator System (RMS). It was the first time the RMS was used to launch satellites, though it had been tested in previous flights. Even though Sally was aware of the pressures on her while she was performing these and other tasks, she showed the calm nerves required of all astronauts, maintaining that "I didn't think so much about the pressure."

Moving objects around in space is nothing like moving objects down on the surface of Earth. With no gravity, objects have no weight, but they still have mass. Mass and weight are different. Mass is the amount of "stuff" in a thing. Weight is the result of gravity pulling on that stuff. If you reduce the gravity, you reduce the amount of pulling. A bowling ball has the

THE CANADARM

The original Remote Manipulator System (RMS) was designed by a company in Canada and is also known as the Canadarm. Five of these arms were built, one for each shuttle, and they were with the shuttle since its first mission in 1981. A new model of the RMS, Canadarm2, was launched with the space shuttle Endeavour in 2001. The new arm is much heavier and a little larger at 4,000 pounds (1,814 kg) and 58 feet (18 m) long. This increase in size makes it stronger, and Canadarm2 can lift larger objects up to 256,000 pounds (116,000 kg). Since the Canadarm2 is used mostly on the International Space Station, it is called the Space Station Remote Manipulator System (SSRMS).

"RIDE SALLY RIDE"

Two songs with the lyrics "Ride Sally Ride" were part of popular culture when Sally Ride rode the space shuttle in 1983—"Mustang Sally," first made popular by Wilson Pickett in 1966, and Lou Reed's "Ride Sally Ride" in 1974. Neither song had anything to do with the astronaut Sally Ride, though she recalls being teased with the song since high school. She also says that she was grateful that neither song was played as a wake-up call on the shuttle! A third pop song does refer to her by name—Billy Joel's "We Didn't Start the Fire" (1989), which Sally recalls being surprised to hear for the first time in her car.

same mass on Earth as on the Moon, but it does not have the same weight, because Earth is pulling the ball downward about six times more than the Moon is.

To lift an object in space, you still have to exert some force even though the objects are weightless. To move a heavy satellite in space, the RMS moves very slowly. By moving slowly, it requires less energy. The RMS moves so slowly that it is hard to see that it is even moving. Although the RMS weighs less than 1,000 pounds (454 kg), it is capable of lifting 65,000 pounds (29,484 kg).

Space Experiments

Besides moving things around with the RMS, Sally helped perform over 40 complicated scientific experiments on Mission STS–7. These experiments had been designed and paid for by scientists who had to remain on Earth. One of them aimed to look at the effect of space on radish seeds.

Some of the experiments Sally performed tested the formation of metal alloys in low gravity. Alloys are mixtures of metals that are combined to improve their properties and make them more suitable for use. For example, iron is a pure metal that rusts easily. By adding a little chromium, another pure metal, an alloy called stainless steel is produced. This alloy is strong, but it does not rust, even though it is mostly iron. Metal alloy research is important for improving all kinds of equipment that is made from metals, such as microchips. Space offers a whole new range of possibilities in the formation of alloys because the different metals stay mixed, without gravity to pull the heavier metals in the mixture down to the bottom.

Having a Little Fun

With all the tasks astronauts have to perform while on their short trips to space, there is little time for anything but work. Sally, however, always made room to have some fun. Crews become a little like family after their long months of training. Long before the week they spend in space, the crew members have spent long days in an intense environment. As it is for all people, a little laughter can help ease stress.

Sally was always one of the crew who lent a touch of the lighthearted to serious situations. In her office at the Johnson Space Center, Sally had a "Pigs in Space" poster on her wall, which featured Miss Piggy from the television program *The Muppet Show*. During a simulation mission that failed, sending the "shuttle" and its crew to what would have been the certain doom of crashing on a beach in Hawaii, Sally offered the cheerful response that all the surfers in the area would be nice enough to come and open the escape hatch for them.

Sally took her sense of humor with her to space. Here is how she described the way in which she and her crewmates improved on the usual astronaut fun experiments with food, such as "drinking" floating drops of orange juice or sending a piece of something sticky flying across the cabin into another crew member's mouth: "We set a cookie floating in the middle of the room and then 'flew' an astronaut, with his mouth wide open, across the cabin to capture it."

When she wasn't working, Sally could usually be found at a window looking down at Earth. She says the experience was "absolutely unbelievable and, unfortunately, indescribable." She does, however, do a pretty good job of describing the view of Earth as "absolutely spectacular, and the feeling of looking back and seeing your planet as a planet is just an amazing feeling. It's a totally different perspective, and it makes you appreciate, actually, how fragile our existence is."

Back to Earth

Cloudy skies in Florida meant the seventh space shuttle mission had to land in California, not at Cape Canaveral, Florida. Instead of the hundreds of thousands of people that had been at the previous touchdowns in Florida, there were fewer than a hundred people in the Mojave Desert runway of Edwards Air Force Base to watch the shuttle's return to Earth. Ironically, Sally's parents had made the trip to Florida to watch their daughter. As it was, she landed 100 miles (161 km) away from her parent's house in California. They could have stayed home! After touchdown, the crew walked around the shuttle where it was

Sally monitors panels near a window on Challenger's *flight deck.*

"You can look at Earth's horizon and see this really, really thin royal blue line right along the horizon, and at first you don't really quite internalize what that is, and then you realize that it's Earth's atmosphere, and that that's all there is of it, and it's about as thick as the fuzz on a tennis ball, and it's everything that separates us from the vacuum of space. If we didn't have that atmosphere, we wouldn't be here, and if we do anything to destroy that atmosphere, we won't be here. So it really puts the planet in perspective."

Sally Ride,
on viewing Earth
from space

parked, and then a few NASA technicians came to greet them. The crew of 300-strong NASA technicians in charge of post-flight activities and tests had to be flown from Florida to California to complete their work.

Then, Sally and her crewmates had to get onto another plane to fly to Houston, where her husband, Steve Hawley, met her and gave her a hug. There was an official ceremony, at which the astronauts stood with their spouses. A NASA official handed Sally a bouquet of flowers in congratulations, but she refused to take it. She was there as an astronaut, not a

After landing, Sally's life changed dramatically for the next few months. She was suddenly very much in the public eye ...

woman. The other astronauts did not receive flowers, so why should she? Sally praised her commander Robert Crippen with these words: "We owe the success of the flight to the Crip." Two thousand people joined her in applause for their mission leader. After the ceremony, Sally's husband ushered her into a car, away from swarms of photographers eager to snap images of America's first woman in space.

NASA claimed it was the best mission yet. President Ronald Reagan had strong praise for

Sally: "You were there for one reason, you were there because you were the best person for the job." After the president's phone call, Sally said at a press conference, "It was fun and I'm sure it will be the most fun I'll ever have in my life." NASA's head of the shuttle program, James Abrahamson, echoed Sally's impressions, "It was clear this whole crew was a happy ship and they did have a good time throughout."

After landing, Sally's life changed dramatically for the next few months. She was suddenly very much in the public eye, although she was not completely comfortable with it. In her own words:

> "I remember a lot of it as very pleasant and, you know, just a set of unbelievable experiences and opportunities to meet people that I'd never imagined being able to meet, and then also something that was very, very difficult for me because I'm happiest when I was in the simulator working with the crew or working with colleagues on a physics problem or playing on a tennis court—not speaking to a group or being the center of attention at a reception or doing TV interviews. It was very, very different for me, and not the way I had envisioned my life."

During this time, Sally and her crewmates visited the White House twice. She sat next to Ronald Reagan during a state dinner, and she went to Europe and met the British ambassador, the King of Norway, and the

Queen of The Netherlands.

It was not until after the shuttle had landed and Sally was out speaking to the public that she realized just what her journey into space had meant to women everywhere. Years later, Sally explained that at first she really didn't think of herself as a "trailblazer" or a "role model," particularly during her training. After all, during that time she was "pretty well insulated by NASA, [who] wanted me training":

"They wanted me to learn what I was supposed to learn. They didn't want me out talking to reporters and the press and the public. So I was not unaware. I read newspapers, I watched television, but I wasn't face to face with women until I came back from my flight, and then it hit home pretty hard how important it was to an awful lot of women in the country."

A Second Mission

More than 18 months after the landing of Mission STS–7, Sally Ride rode up in the *Challenger* again. The date was October 5, 1984, and it was the 13th time a shuttle had flown into space. The mission was STS–41G, and it, too, had several firsts. It was the first time seven crew members were on the shuttle, and it was the first time a Canadian, Marc Garneau, was in space. NASA astronaut Kathryn (Kate) Sullivan was also among the crew, which placed two women in space on one shuttle at the same time. This mission also marked Kate Sullivan becoming the first

MORE WOMEN IN SPACE

Throughout the 1990s, women continued to prove that space is not just a man's domain. Eileen Collins was an inspiration to many when she sat behind the controls of the *Discovery* and became the first woman to pilot a space shuttle in 1995. Two missions later, she launched in the *Columbia* as flight commander—another first. In 2008, the 25th anniversary year of Sally's flight, astronaut Karen Nyberg became the 50th woman in space. In April 2010, Mission STS–131 launched with three women aboard. With another female astronaut already in orbit aboard the International Space Station, this event placed the most women in space at one time.

The official NASA portrait of STS–93 commander Eileen M. Collins, shown wearing a launch and entry suit (LES) and holding her helmet.

"The first few months after my flight I was really struck by the way that women of all ages—from college students to 60-year-old, 70-year-old, 80-year-old women—reacted to me. It was just something that they never thought they would see. And it made quite an impression on me."

Sally Ride, on the impact of her historic mission on other women woman to do a space walk. During her walk, she was outside the space shuttle in a space suit for three and a half hours. The purpose of this space walk was to demonstrate that a satellite could be refueled. The commander for Mission STS–41G was Robert Crippen, who'd also led Sally's first trip into space.

> "On both of my flights, everything went very well."
>
> Sally Ride

In addition to the satellite refueling trial, the main tasks for the crew involved the launch and maintenance of several satellites. The first one was successfully put in place using the robotic arm less than nine hours into the flight. Mission STS–41G also had several experiments related to monitoring and recording data from Earth. One of the satellites launched measured the Sun's energy reaching Earth. Other experiments in the shuttle itself involved the taking of large-format photos of our planet, measuring air pollution, taking climate readings, and observing the oceans. The *Challenger* was in space for 197.5 hours (over eight days) before landing at the Kennedy Space Center in Florida, on October 13. It was the last time Sally Ride would leave the safety of Earth's atmosphere.

Above: Astronauts Kathryn D. Sullivan, left, and Sally K. Ride display a "bag of worms." The "bag" is a sleep restraint, and the "worms" are its springs and clips.

Left: The Mission STS–41G insignia

Chapter 5
73 Seconds That Changed Everything

O n the morning of January 28, 1986, the
space shuttle *Challenger* stood ready
on the launch pad at Cape Canaveral,
Florida. Members of its ground crew were
going through final system checks. At 11:38
a.m., Mission Control gave the go-ahead, and
the main engines started. As was normal,
shock waves rippled through the shuttle's
hull and into the seats of the seven astronauts
aboard. The shuttle lifted into the sky.

A Liftoff Unlike Any Other

This was going to be a special day for NASA.
Three years before, Sally Ride was the first
female astronaut to fly into space, and today
was to mark the first time an American civilian
would go up. On board the *Challenger* was
Christa McAuliffe, a schoolteacher from New
Hampshire and the first participant in NASA's
Teach in Space Program. The plan was that
she would teach two lessons while orbiting
Earth. NASA hoped that a successful space
flight with a civilian would develop public
confidence in the space shuttle as a transport
vehicle. Many classrooms around the world
were watching live as the event of the launch
unfolded. Television sets had been wheeled into

classrooms, and people paused in shopping malls before TV stores. Millions of eyes were on the launch.

About 500 spectators had gathered for the launch, including Christa's parents, and a small group of young children from Christa's hometown of Concord, New Hampshire. Sally had been to space twice before and was in training for a third mission. At this time, she was enjoying her career as America's pioneer female astronaut. She was a perfect image of what NASA wanted in their men and women in space.

"A Major Malfunction"

A puff of smoke appeared above the trees, and the shuttle, distant and just visible, gently rose above the ground on a column of white-hot flame. The crowd clapped, children waved small flags, and Christa's parents hugged and congratulated each other. Then, over the loudspeaker transmitting the communications between the shuttle and Mission Control, the launch spectators hear the words, "Flight controllers here looking very carefully at the situation. Obviously a major malfunction."

At 11:39 a.m., 73 seconds after liftoff, the unthinkable happened. The *Challenger* exploded. There had been no warning to those on the ground. Those in front of television screens saw a brief flash as the lower end was momentarily engulfed in flames. Then, the shuttle broke up, its remains nothing more than small pieces trailing smoke and raining down into the Atlantic Ocean. More than 48,000 feet (14,630 meters) above the Atlantic

A close-up view of the liftoff of the space shuttle Challenger *on January 28, 1986. The circle in the lower right corner of the photo shows a cloud of smoke on the right side of the solid rocket booster directly across from the letter "U" in "United States." This smoke was the first visible sign of a leak from a joint between the sections of the solid rocket booster. Hot gases escaped from the joint, ultimately causing a massive explosion. All seven* Challenger *crew members were killed.*

Ocean, the *Challenger* had broken apart, killing all seven people on board.

Four of the astronauts killed in the *Challenger* explosion were members of Sally's astronaut class, which was recruited in 1977. She had worked with them for eight years. Sally describes her reaction to the accident and the loss that went with it:

> *"I'd worked with them every day, I'd gone to dinner at their houses, I knew their families. So they were very, very close, close friends. My then husband had been on the flight before the* Challenger *accident, and I was scheduled to go about two months after the* Challenger *accident. So it hit me very personally, just to lose friends and to think about what might have been."*

As the personal and national grieving unfolded in the days and weeks to come, one stunning reality came into focus: Instead of providing public faith in space exploration, the death of Christa and her fellow crew members caused people to wonder if space exploration was worth the risk.

The Dangers of Space Flight

The shuttles that travel into space endure an incredible amount of physical stress. When a shuttle takes off, every nut and bolt is pushed, pulled, and twisted as the spacecraft is shot into the air. When the shuttle's mission is finished, and it is headed back to Earth, the craft slams into Earth's atmosphere while

During the Challenger explosion, pieces of the orbiter, including parts of the left wing and engines, leave trails of smoke as they hurtle through the sky.

Crew members of ill-fated space shuttle Mission STS–51L pose for their official portrait on November 15, 1985. In the back row from left to right: Ellison S. Onizuka, Christa McAuliffe, Gregory Jarvis, and Judith Resnik. In the front row from left to right: Michael J. Smith, Dick Scobee, and Ronald McNair.

traveling at 18,000 miles per hour (28,968 km/h). At such an incredible speed the shuttle is shaken, rattled, bounced, and subjected to incredible heat. When people moving at 60 miles per hour (100 km/h) in a car stick their hands out the windows, they feel force pushing against them. Imagine the force against an object traveling at 18,000 miles per hour!

The space shuttle must be maintained as a finely tuned machine to withstand these incredible forces. It does not take much to upset the balance. To minimize the danger of space flight, NASA spends far more time on training than actual missions. Astronauts train for months or years for a mission that may last less than a week. Even with all the safety checks and training, space exploration is still a very risky profession because of the simple fact that space is a difficult place to get to.

The President Wants Answers

The recovery of pieces of the exploded shuttle started within minutes of the breakup. Twenty percent of STS–51L was recovered and the pieces sent to NASA's warehouses, where they could be sorted and examined. With the world asking how this could happen, President Ronald Reagan created a group called the Rogers Commission to investigate the event for the president. Sally Ride was also chosen by the president to be one of 13 commissioners.

The commission's first task was to ask questions. They employed many scientists and technicians to analyze the disaster and do tests on the *Challenger* remains. For six months they looked at every fragment recovered and analyzed it. They conducted interviews with NASA and Thiokol staff, and they examined training methods. Sally Ride was responsible for evaluating both the mission planning and leading causes of the disaster. They were O-ring failure in low temperatures and poor decision making by officials of NASA and Thiokol—the company that builds the shuttle's solid rocket boosters—who were aware of possible disaster and took the risk anyway.

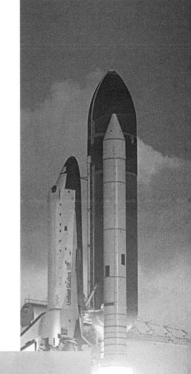

Becoming "Operational"

Newly designed and built airplanes must be tested on hundreds of flights before passengers are allowed to ride them. Only then are they considered operational. The space shuttle, in spite of its complexity, did not go through this process. "Everyone thought we were operational, and we were not," says John Young, Chief of the Astronaut Office. Instead, the space shuttle only had four test flights. The fifth flight carried mission specialists and, by the 12th, it was carrying payload specialists, who are not trained in flying the shuttle. NASA treated each mission as a test flight, carefully examining the shuttle on its return for anything that might show where improvements were needed. Sally Ride went up in the shuttle's seventh flight and, by date of the last scheduled space shuttle mission, September 2010, NASA had only attempted 134 flights in total.

Explaining the Accident

Looking back through the records of launch and testing data, the commission found one piece of information that kept showing up: damaged O-rings. Since the first test launch of the solid rocket boosters in 1981, there had been 15 launches during which O-ring failure was noted. There had only been nine launches without any O-ring damage. This is not a very good track record.

A few flights before, on Mission STS–51C, rocket engineers detected evidence that hot gases had escaped through the joints between the segments of the rockets. Evidence of a leak was found when the rockets were examined after completion of the mission. The engineers looked for the cause and found that low temperatures, about 51 °F (11 °C), on launch day had resulted in the leak. The temperature on January 28 was even colder: 31 °F (-1 °C).

Examination of the *Challenger* wreckage and the photos and film taken of the launch told the full story. The morning of the *Challenger* disaster was so cold that the O-rings had shrunk to open up a gap less than the thickness of a human hair. At about 50 seconds after liftoff, severe side winds high in the atmosphere slammed into the shuttle and forced it off course. The onboard computers automatically steered the shuttle back on course. The strain on the shuttle caused the joint to open up, and the damaged O-rings could do nothing to stop the flood of super-heated gases from escaping. The heated gases pointed directly at the external fuel tank. The fuel tank was ruptured, releasing thousands of gallons of

SOLID ROCKET BOOSTERS, JOINTS, AND O-RINGS

At launch, the two 150-foot- (46 m) tall white solid rocket boosters attached to either side of the large orange fuel tank provide most of the lift that allows the shuttle to get away from Earth. They are not built in one long piece, but in shorter sections that are bolted together. These sections have complicated joints where they meet that must withstand the high pressure and temperature of the gases inside. O-rings are rings of rubber, like giant rubber bands going around each section of rocket. There are two of them at each joint. A similar construction is used when two garden hoses are screwed together. A rubber O-ring keeps the joint between the hoses tight. If the O-ring used in a garden hose is damaged or not squeezed tightly enough, water will spray out. The hot gases engineers detected on the solid rocket boosters of Mission STS–51C had leaked past the O-rings in the same way.

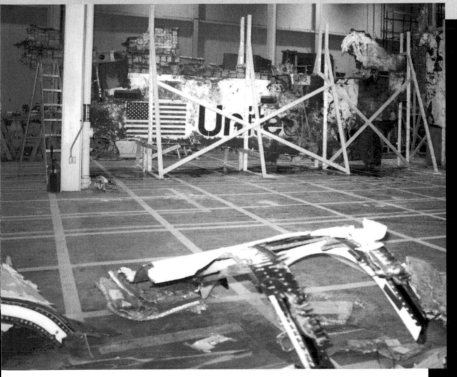

Debris recovered from the Challenger *and brought to the Kennedy Space Center was studied by investigation teams. Taped squares on the floor formed a grid used to help place the pieces in their original places, like a puzzle with many pieces missing.*

liquid hydrogen, which ignited. The resulting explosion tore the shuttle to pieces.

The commission members had their answer to how the *Challenger* accident happened, but now they needed to know why. If the problem with the O-rings was known to exist before the launch, why was it not corrected?

Risks Ignored

At 11:45 p.m., the night before the disaster, Thiokol engineer Roger Boisjoly slammed pictures down in front of his managers. He felt he was being ignored, and he was angry. The two pictures were of recovered rockets that had sent the *Discovery* to space the year before. "You have to be blind, deaf, and dumb not to know what these two pictures are telling you," Roger Boisjoly told the Thiokol managers seated before him, pointing to the burned O-rings in the photos.

The managers of Thiokol did not want to be the ones to cancel the launch, however. They didn't like what Roger was trying to tell them. The news was not good, but was it so bad that they had to tell NASA not to launch? NASA was behind schedule already, and putting off the launch would waste a lot of time and money. NASA was Thiokol's biggest client, and as one of the managers said to Boisjoly, "Just remember that the customer is always right." NASA pressured the managers at Thiokol to get a green light. Thiokol got it; Mission STS–51L was a go.

Does this make Thiokol to blame? In risky situations, companies generally must prove that the environment they put their employees in is safe. Sally Ride found that the opposite was true in NASA: "Engineers who wanted to postpone the shuttle launch were effectively, they felt, required to prove a safety problem. Normally, it's just the reverse." Though Roger Boisjoly's images of burned O-rings proved there was a defect in the design, he could not prove that the shuttle would certainly explode if it was launched. That was all the managers needed to hear. They gave NASA the thumbs up with the condition that they wait for the temperature to warm up a bit. After helping with the investigation into the cause of the disaster, Sally knew the "accident" was not entirely accidental. In her words, "as the investigation unfolded, it became very clear that that system had broken down, and that that system that we trusted to track down any flaw or any piece of bad test data really had failed."

The *Challenger* disaster changed space exploration forever. NASA stopped its shuttle program altogether for almost three years. When it started up again, things were different. Prior to 1986, NASA had been running 12 or more missions a year. This number was cut in half when the shuttle program resumed. Many of the people closely involved with the disaster chose a new path for themselves. Roger quit working for Thiokol, and Sally switched from being an active astronaut to being involved with the planning of missions. She would never ride in a shuttle again.

Chapter 6
Lessons for the Future

In the years following the *Challenger* disaster, Sally Ride explored many careers. She spent a year at NASA as an advisor on future projects. She researched the problem of nuclear weapons at Stanford University and suggested a way the planet's nations could peacefully do away with them. She even spent time working for an Internet company that focused on getting science news out of the laboratories and to the public. Through all the changes, Sally continued to explore ideas, communicate, and build partnerships.

Guiding NASA

During the Rogers Commission, Sally still occupied her desk in NASA's Johnson Space

Sally felt that by focusing on exploration, leadership in space exploration could bring renewed interest in NASA and global leadership for the United States.

Center. After that, Sally's crewmates from her previous two missions entered training again, but Sally instead moved to NASA headquarters in Washington, D.C., away from the training facility and away from the action. Here, she led the new Office of Exploration and Office of Strategic Planning. Her job was to address the "long-term direction of the U.S. civilian space program."

Sally's new position put her in a place of great importance in influencing the future of the U.S. space program. She was worried that during the first five years of shuttle missions, the space program had become increasingly commercial. The shuttles were flying more often and with less attention to safety. The original purpose of space travel—to research the physical universe beyond the surface of Earth—was no longer a top priority.

NASA's reasons for this change were simple. Space exploration is very expensive. Each satellite NASA launched for a company or government meant dollars in its pocket to help pay for the space program. For Sally, however, the research spirit of the 1960s and 1970s had been lost along the way. NASA did not seem interested in going beyond the routine visits to low-orbit. The Soviet Union, on the other hand, had put eight space stations into orbit since the mid-1970s. Sally saw this as a loss of leadership, which also led to a loss of interest by the public, who no longer watched NASA activities on TV to any great extent. Sally felt that by focusing on exploration, leadership in space exploration could bring renewed interest in NASA and global leadership for the United States.

SPACE STATIONS

A permanent space station allows for the continual presence of astronauts and scientists in space. Experiments can last months and the long-term effects of zero gravity can be better understood. The Soviet Union led the way in the development of an orbiting space station. After several short-lived attempts, assembly of the space station Mir started in 1986. Mir was built in seven sections, and was completed in 1996. The station could comfortably house three people on long-term stays and up to six people for short periods. Before the project was ended in 2001, people had been living in Mir nearly ten years!

The International Space Station (ISS) is truly an international effort with components supplied by 16 different countries. Construction started in 1998 and, by November 2000, the ISS has had crews living permanently aboard. Primarily a research facility, crews conduct research into biology, physics, astronomy, and meteorology. Completed in 2011, the ISS will continue to be in operation until 2020.

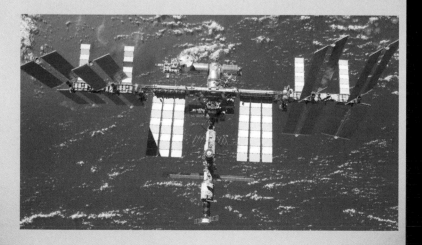

With Earth providing a backdrop, the International Space Station is seen in this photo taken by a crew member of the space shuttle Endeavour *during Mission STS–130.*

The *Ride Report*

In 1987, Sally produced a report with the title *NASA Leadership and America's Future in Space: A Report to the Administrator*. This report also had another, unofficial name: the *Ride Report*. This 65-page document outlined what Sally saw as NASA's future in four stages: Mission to Planet Earth, Exploration of the Solar System, Outpost on the Moon, and Humans to Mars.

Mission to Planet Earth

The purpose of Sally's proposed Mission to Planet Earth was to "obtain a comprehensive scientific understanding of the entire Earth System, by describing how its various components function, how they interact, and how they may be expected to evolve" in the future. Sally hoped NASA would accomplish this with four satellites that took measurements from orbit. Sally suggested that it would take decades to collect the needed data. While this project was never acted upon, Sally did anticipate the environmental sciences that developed during the 1990s in response to climate change.

Exploration of the Solar System

Exploration of the Solar System would "continue the quest to understand our planetary system, its origin, and its evolution." Not since 1976 had a U.S. mission visited the planet Mars. Sally hoped NASA would change this, and she even stated that the mission "would bring a handful of Mars back to Earth before the year 2000." In Sally's plan, Saturn

The Mars Global Surveyor was launched in 1996 and has orbited Mars for many years. It has provided large amounts of information about Mars' atmosphere and surface, as well as information about the Martian moon Phobos. This is an artist's impression of what the surveyor might look like, circling above Mars.

Artist John J. Olson's impression of the future of space exploration: a base on Mars.

JOHN J. OLSON

would also be visited, as would a comet and an asteroid. While NASA never developed a method to land on Saturn, the Mars Global Surveyor (MGS) entered Mars' orbit in 1997 and took measurements and images for two years. There have been several landings since, but none has attempted to return to Earth with a handful of dirt. Instead, the Mars landers had sophisticated equipment that analyzed the surface and sent back data.

Outpost on the Moon

Outpost on the Moon was a project to "land astronauts on the lunar surface in the year 2000, to construct an outpost that would evolve in size and capability and would be a vital, visible extension of our capabilities and our vision." Sally saw humans on the Moon as pioneers "pitching their tents" and learning to "live off the land." In Sally's plan, NASA would use robots to search the surface for a suitable site then, by 2000, they would have the first base set up. Five years later, there would be permanent inhabitants.

Humans on Mars

Humans on Mars was Sally's most ambitious plan. She envisioned a permanent settlement on the red planet by 2015:

"A successful Mars initiative would recapture the high ground of world space leadership and would provide an exciting focus for creativity, motivation, and pride of the American people. The challenge is compelling, and it is enormous."

Sadly, the public considered Sally's vision as impossible, dangerous, and expensive. At a time when NASA's budget was shrinking, Sally was suggesting increasing spending to such an amount that many people said that if she had her way, she would bankrupt the agency.

Protection from Above

In the same year that Sally finished the *Ride Report*, two major changes occurred in her life. For one, she and Steve Hawley divorced. They had no children. Secondly, she officially retired from NASA. She would continue to cooperate with the space agency on many projects, but it was time for her to change direction: "I had always had it in the back of my head that I wanted to do research and to teach at a university. So it was natural for me to come back to the university after the space program."

Sally's next obvious choice would be to complete what is called postdoctoral research, or a "postdoc." A postdoc is research work done to further increase a person's expertise in a particular field. Depending on the school and the field of study, some universities require that a postdoc be completed before the person can be hired as a professor.

Sally completed her postdoc at the Center for International Security and Arms Control (CISAC) at Stanford University from 1987 to 1988. CISAC is a group of professors from various subjects such as science, political studies, and engineering. They are all working toward a more secure and peaceful future by looking at issues of international security and modern weaponry.

A U.S. Air Force missile systems analyst inspects an LGM–30G Minuteman III missile inside a missile silo at Grand Forks Air Force Base, North Dakota, in 1989.

With CISAC, Sally Ride was able to research something that had been of interest her entire professional career: the relationship between space and space exploration, and national security. Space is important to security because nuclear warheads are not set off by soldiers in muddy fields or fired from tanks. Modern nuclear weapons are space weapons. They fly hundreds of miles higher than even the space shuttle before falling on their targets. Sally felt it was her responsibility to put her knowledge of space to use to assist in the nuclear disarming of the world's nations. Sally wanted to work toward peace.

The two years that Sally was with CISAC and worked on the problems of nuclear weapons took place during a period known as the Cold War. Without actually fighting, tensions between United States and the Soviet Union made war between the two countries a possible, or even likely,

MINUTEMAN MISSILES

Simmering tensions between the United States and the Soviet Union during the Cold War created a need for missiles to carry nuclear warheads. The United States created the Minuteman missile to fulfill this need. Between 1960 and 1965, 800 of these missiles were produced and made ready, each loaded with a 1.2-megaton nuclear warhead. This size of warhead can destroy an area of 10 square miles (26 sq km). By 1967, the Minuteman II had been developed. It could carry two warheads and travel greater distances, and it was far more accurate.

Both Minuteman and Minuteman II missiles were liquid fueled, which meant they had to be "gassed up" before launching. In the event of nuclear attack, there would not be time to launch them. The Minuteman III solved this problem. Designed in 1970, it used solid fuel and could be fired instantly from a remote launch control center.

Today, there are 450 Minuteman III missiles powered up and ready to launch by the U.S. Army. Each missile is capable of traveling 8,100 miles (13,360 km) at speeds of 15,000 miles per hour (24,140 KPH). When launched, the engines propel the missile to an altitude of over 700 miles (1,127 km), which is over four times the average height of a space shuttle mission. The warheads then drop to Earth without the aid of engines. At a cost of $7 million each, the Army is not making any more Minuteman IIIs, but will maintain the ones it has until they are retired in 2030.

event in people's minds. While Sally had been training to be an astronaut, the United States and the Soviet Union were rivals in several arenas. One of them, as we have seen, was space, but they were also in an arms race. The two countries were competing with one another to build a bigger collection of weapons—nuclear weapons.

In an attempt to resolve the arms race, Sally concentrated on one solution: banning all nuclear weapons. This solution to the problem might sound simple, but it was far from it. By 1987, the two countries had signed an agreement to begin the process of reducing the number of nuclear weapons. At this point, there were tens of thousands of these weapons and nobody could agree how to start the process.

First of all, the two nations had to agree on how many weapons they had. Neither government wanted to open their doors and allow the other side to poke around inside their weapons sheds, but neither side would trust the other to just tell them how many they had. Sally provided each side with a method to monitor its opponent's weapon systems and, in so doing, she was paving the way to the end of the Cold War.

Today, nuclear bombs are not very big— about the size and shape of a large coffee thermos. The missiles that deliver nuclear bombs to their targets, on the other hand, are huge. The missiles in use by the United States stand about 60 feet (18 m) high and weigh about 78,000 pounds (35,380 kg). At the time, people feared that nuclear warheads could be carried around in secret and inserted into missiles that were considered to be ordinary, non-nuclear weapons. Sally outlined the following three steps to be used by the United States and the Soviet Union to control the loading of warheads into ordinary missiles:

1) Each country would keep a list of all the missiles the other country owned. A scientist would inspect each of the missiles and test them to make sure they did not hold a nuclear device.

2) Each missile would have a special tag attached to it. Since each missile looks just like the one next to it, a tag would act like a fingerprint so missiles could not be switched or moved around to hide them from inspectors. Sally described the perfect tag as "durable and tamper-proof."

3) Each missile would be sealed shut. If the missile was opened and a warhead installed, the inspector would be able to tell at once. Sally's idea was to use a fiber optic mesh to cover the door. This material would be impossible to copy, and a special device could be created to "read" the mesh and determine whether it had been altered.

Sally's plan was a needed step in the direction of world peace. Not long after she produced her report, the two sides began a process of inspection that continues to this day. There are still nuclear arms in the hands of many world powers, but the fear of nuclear attack is less because the different countries are more open about what weapons they have.

With her research published, Sally Ride's post-doc was complete, and she was ready to

start looking for a permanent job as a professor. She found it at an excellent research university, the University of California at San Diego (UCSD).

Professorship

Sally Ride began her job as a physics professor at UCSD in the fall of 1989. It was the start of a new phase in her life, very different from her years working with NASA. As a professor, she was now free to explore any question that interested her. As Sally explains:

"My research interests center on the theory of nonlinear beam-wave interactions, primarily connected with free electron lasers and related nonlinear systems."

If this sounds a little complicated, that's because it is! Some of Sally's research goes into depth about such sophisticated-sounding topics as proton gyrofrequency, ponderomotive forces, and parametric interactions.

Bow Shocks

Simply put, Sally studies what happens in space when something very small meets up with something very large. The results of these encounters are called bow shocks. Bow shocks tell astronomers a great deal about stars, planets, and the forces that surround them, so it is important that scientists understand what they are and what causes them.

When solar wind—the stream of particles given off by stars—moves past a planet, or

Space Particles

There are many gigantic objects in outer space such as planets and stars. The space between these large bodies is not empty, but filled with a lot of very small particles. Collected together, all of these small particles are called the interstellar medium. There is a lot of it. In every cubic meter of outer space, a cube about the size of a school desk, there are about one million particles. These particles are so small that if you put them all in a pile, you would not be able to see that pile. In fact, you would need about 100 million particles of interstellar space to create a small dot on a page.

These interstellar space particles are gas and dust atoms and molecules. They are left over from the formation of the galaxy and the explosions of old stars. They provide information that scientists like Sally can use in the study of the origins of stars, planets, galaxies, and even the building blocks of life here on Earth.

Sally also studies another source of small particles in space: solar wind. Solar wind is a stream of particles that is given off by stars, including the Sun. Like the heat from a fire, solar wind consists of particles that are even smaller than atoms.

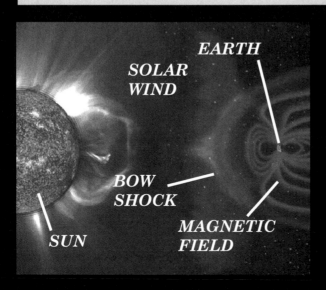

EARTH

SOLAR WIND

BOW SHOCK

SUN

MAGNETIC FIELD

An artist's concept of the Sun's solar wind hitting Earth. The circular patterns around Earth show Earth's magnetic field. The larger curved shape shows the bow shock created as the solar wind is deflected around Earth by the magnetic field. Solar wind causes magnetic storms that can disrupt our communications, damage satellites, and cause electrical blackouts.

when a star plows through an assortment of matter in space known as the interstellar medium, a bow shock occurs. Bow shocks are similar to the effect of water flowing past an object in its path. In a river, water must move to either side to get around a boulder before continuing on its way downstream. In space, stars and planets act like large boulders in a fast-flowing stream of the interstellar medium or solar wind.

The region where the interstellar medium or solar wind is turned aside is called the bow shock. Earth's bow shock is about 43,000 miles (69,202 km) above our heads. The bow shock of some stars and planets is visible through very powerful telescopes. A bow shock looks like a gently curved line, like the line of a wave in front of a boat plowing through the water. The shape of a star's bow shock gives astronomers information about how fast a star is traveling through space. The extent of a planet's bow shock provides information about how magnetic the planet is.

Another Tragedy

In 2003, almost exactly 17 years after the *Challenger* disaster, Sally was happily installed at UCSD in her research and teaching. A new generation of astronauts and ground crews were putting space shuttles into orbit when, what had been "the unthinkable" up to 1986, happened again. At 3:39 in the afternoon on January 16, *Columbia* lifted off for Mission STS–107 without difficulty. Eighty-three seconds into the flight, a chunk of orange foam about the size of a couch cushion broke off the

Columbia *lifts off on its final mission. The light-colored triangle circled to the left of Columbia's nose cone is a piece of insulating material that broke off of the external fuel tank at about 82 seconds into the flight. The piece damaged part of the shuttle's left wing, causing Columbia's destruction upon re-entry several days later.*

outside of the external fuel tank. The piece struck the wing of Columbia and damaged the covering of the shuttle that protects it from extreme heat during re-entry.

Something as alarming as pieces falling off at launch may sound like a huge problem, but it had happened many times before without causing major damage. This time, however, the outcome would prove disastrous.

Strapped in their seats, the crew had no idea their shuttle was slowly going to pieces.

On February 1, at 8:15 a.m., the *Columbia* was given the go-ahead to begin its descent to Earth. For the first 30 minutes, the entry went as planned but, at 8:48 a.m., a sensor in the left wing of *Columbia* alerted the crew that the wing was under more strain than ever encountered before. Five minutes later, the shuttle crossed over California, traveling at 15,000 miles per hour (24,000 KPH). It was 43 miles (69 km) away from Earth, but people on the ground saw numerous streaks of light similar to a meteor. They knew something was wrong. The flashes of light they saw were small pieces of the shuttle slowly breaking loose and burning up. Strapped in their seats, the crew had no idea their shuttle was slowly going to pieces.

At 9:00 a.m., thousands of people in Texas watched the *Columbia's* final moments. These witnesses saw a few streaks of brilliant light and then nothing.

When *Columbia* broke apart on February 1, 2003, killing its seven-member crew and scattering debris for miles, people were asking themselves: Is this the *Challenger* all over again?

A memorial service was held three days later. Sally Ride was appearing at a science festival. As an astronaut, she knew the risks of space travel. But she also knew that she and all of the astronauts were committed to the space program and forwarding scientific discovery. She discussed the *Columbia* disaster with these words, "We'll pick up the torch the astronauts carried and carry it forward."

Another Investigation

Not long after Sally Ride heard the news of the *Columbia* disaster, NASA contacted her to tell her she had been chosen to sit on the *Columbia* Accident Investigation Board (CAIB). Seventeen years had passed since Sally had been asked to investigate the destruction of a shuttle and its crew, and now she had to go through the process all over again.

Sadly, the investigation found the same management problems that had led to the *Challenger* accident years before. In both situations, even though NASA was aware of a problem, they did little more than cross their fingers and hope for the best. Since the problem with foam pieces breaking off during liftoff had never caused major damage, it was ignored. Sally recognized that it is human nature to become used to a situation. If something happens often enough, it seems normal, even if it is risky. Sally explained:"

"Counting the Apollo 1 *fire, there have been three major NASA accidents, each of them almost a generation apart. The problem is, people forget. The lessons of* Challenger, *for instance, were on everyone's minds at NASA for several years after that accident. Then some people retired. New people came in. Seventeen years passed. Over the years, a lot of things crept into the system without people's noticing."*

Sally's view is that while some of the choices NASA management made in the past are regrettable, space travel will always entail the risk of loss of human life. The task for NASA is to continually minimize those risks. Sally said following the *Columbia* disaster:

"The shuttle launched successfully 112 times and failed twice. That's a very good record for a launch vehicle. That's a bad record for anything that carries people."

After the *Columbia* disaster investigation, Sally carried on her duties as a professor. In 2010, she was still a professor at UCSD, although she has taken a leave from studying bow shocks to concentrate on solving a problem closer to Earth: science education.

CHALLENGER STS 51-L ★ JANUARY 28, 1986
FRANCIS "DICK" SCOBEE, MICHAEL J. SMITH, JUDITH A. RESNIK, ELLISON S. ONIZUKA
RONALD E. McNAIR, GREGORY B. JARVIS, S. CHRISTA McAULIFFE

COLUMBIA STS-107 ★ FEBRUARY 1, 2003
LAUREL BLAIR SALTON CLARK, DAVID M. BROWN, MICHAEL P. ANDERSON, ILAN RAMON
RICK D. HUSBAND, WILLIAM C. McCOOL, KALPANA CHAWLA

A portion of a plaque laid at the Astronaut's Memorial at the Kennedy Space Center in memory of the astronauts who died in the Challenger *and* Columbia *disasters*

Chapter 7
Science Is for Girls

Other than bow shocks, something else attracted Sally's attention while she was a professor. Sally noticed that there were not many girls taking her courses.

KidSat

It was this observation in her university classrooms that led to Sally's concern for the future of science as a field that would be continually dominated by men. Sally wanted to make sure that girls are allowed the same opportunities she had in science to pursue their interests.

Sally embarked on a program in 1995 to encourage young people, especially girls, to stay interested in science as they grow older. To accomplish this, Sally wanted to get students excited about learning. She came up with the idea to use NASA's space program to tap into the natural curiosity of youth. The outcome was KidSat.

She came up with the idea to use NASA's space program to tap into the natural curiosity of youth.

KidSat put school kids behind the controls of a camera aboard the space shuttle. From their classroom, kids logged in and directed the camera to take pictures of Earth and to take readings on conditions in the atmosphere. In effect, KidSat was "giving students their own piece of the space program," says Sally.

The camera used for KidSat was made by Kodak specifically for the project. It was pre-programmed by Sally and her team at UCSD according to the targets sent to her by interested school groups. Sally then sent the programming on to NASA to load onto the shuttle's computers. Once this was done, the kids were taking part in a real NASA mission.

After a few successful test runs on space shuttle missions STS–76, –81, and –86 in 1996 and 1997, the project was considered such a success it was renamed EarthKAM. It flew on two more shuttles, but Sally was not satisfied with that. Shuttle trips were too infrequent and only lasted a few days. In 1998, the International Space Station was under construction, and Sally hoped her requests for a permanent camera there would be granted.

On a typical mission, such as ISS 10–02, there were 139 schools participating in EarthKAM. Over 1,500 photographs were taken of Earth, and the students using them learned about geography, math, environmental sciences, and much more in real-world situations and, perhaps more importantly, in situations of their own design.

This ability to ask their own questions and get answers had Sally hoping students would remember the experience and pursue science in school. Perhaps participants would even consider a career in science, too. Sally's love of science is infectious, and no doubt her attitude spills over. "It's amazing that people can make a career out of asking questions," Sally said.

Space.com

With EarthKAM operating successfully, Sally went searching for another opportunity to communicate science to youth and the public. With the growing interest in the Internet, she got involved with an online company called Space.com, becoming president of the company in the winter of 1999. In a short time, her contributions had led to a print magazine and partnerships with organizations such as NASA. Space.com is still going strong. It features a collection of science news, space exploration history, and a gathering place for people interested in space.

Around this time, Sally started to think that she should turn her attentions away from helping others, like Space.com, reach their goals and instead reach the goals she herself felt most passionate about—"finding ways to keep girls interested in science."

"There have been many women in space, but I'm the one that people remember. That gives me a major responsibility to talk to girls, to young women— to help them appreciate that these are careers that are wide open for women."

Sally Ride

"You walk into a classroom and ask if anybody has a question and everybody's hand goes up. It doesn't matter what the subject is. Just by taking advantage of that natural curiosity, you can start them on a path toward scientific literacy and appreciating that these are interesting topics."

In May of 2000, Sally left Space.com. "It has been an exciting 15 months, with an exciting company," Sally said, but she found she needed to follow her own path. She said that breaking with the company gave her a chance to put her energies in an area that's very important to her. This energy has resulted in a company, formed in 2001, that has flourished ever since. It has put Sally in the position she always wanted to be in—making a difference to young girls. Sally called her company Sally Ride Science.

Sally Ride Science

Urey Hall is a plain concrete building that was built in 1963, the same year Valentina Tereshkova became the first woman in space. It is here that Sally has her office on the campus of UCSD, and here that she developed her plans for Sally Ride Science. Her aim is to encourage girls in science when they are still young and naturally curious. When Sally goes out and talks to classrooms of fourth-grade kids, just as many girls want to be astronauts as do boys. Yet, as a university professor, she sees mostly boys in her classes.

"What happened to those fourth-grade girls?" Sally wants to know. As the system encourages males, even boys who only get C's in math, to be very confident, "all these girls who get A's in math ... say, 'I'm not good enough.'"

Sally blames this situation on age-old stereotypes, peer pressure, and other elements of our society, but she hopes to help change all that.

Sally Ride Science has two goals: to inspire young girls to become interested in science and to change society's perception that technology is for boys. Sally Ride Science organizes space camps and science festivals, publishes books on exciting careers for girls, and creates fun and innovative materials for teachers to use in the classroom. It also develops and runs contests, like the Toy Design Challenge.

Girls need to know that the world of science belongs to all of us and that natural curiosity about the universe is appropriate for girls as well as boys. Sally's hope is that, by building a community of young female students excited about science, they will be able to overcome stereotypes.

How did Sally herself overcome these stereotypes growing up? "I picked my parents well," Sally said laughing. She points out that her parents always encouraged her interest in science, even though they were not scientists themselves. They bought her a microscope and took her to science museums. Sally also feels that being in an all-girls school was very important. "Everyone in trig [math] class was a girl. Everyone in chemistry was a girl." By not having to share a classroom with boys, the girls also did not have to share their excitement. In addition, Sally had her female role models:

"I was inspired by one of my female science teachers—an accomplished researcher with a degree in physiology."

Shortly after Sally Ride Science became a success, Sally put her career at UCSD on hold to dedicate more time to her work with youth. Now she spends two to three months of the year away from home, visiting schools and attending events. On the road, Sally's part in the Sally Ride Science company is to speak to kids at science festivals and motivate them. She gives a keynote address, showing slides and talking about what it's like to be an astronaut. She and her group also arrange a street fair with such attractions as DJs playing music, food, and loads of exhibits, booths, and workshops run by female professionals, "ranging from veterinarians to aerospace engineers."

While all this sounds very exciting, Sally does not really like the travel part of her life. Perhaps when you have flown in a space shuttle around Earth, flying from city to city is not very exciting. When she arrives in a new city, she tends to stick close to her hotel room and gets ready for the event rather than hitting the streets to see the sights.

If there is one place that Sally allows herself to linger while traveling, it is the National Air and Space Museum in Washington, D.C. "I can't help myself. If I've got a little bit of time, I always start there and never make it out. My favorite is the Apollo capsules, but I stay away from any exhibits that mention me. That's very weird."

This photo, taken in September 2008, shows a group of San Francisco Bay Area girls at NASA Research Park in California. NASA's Ames Research Center collaborated with Sally Ride Science to sponsor and host the Sally Ride Science Festival, a fun-filled day of interactive exploration of science, technology, engineering, and mathematics.

This dislike of seeing her own name celebrated has always been a big part of Sally's character. It's not because Sally is shy. After all, she gets up every few days and speaks to audiences of thousands of strangers. Sally is just very careful about how she uses her fame. For example, there is no authorized biography written about her—she has not allowed one. Why? Because she feels she has not yet done enough with her life. Perhaps Sally has a lot more she wants to do in the next few decades.

Sally Ride's Legacy

Sally Ride has a lot to say to youth, to women, to her country, and to the world. Much of her message lies in the attitudes and actions she has taken in her own life, such as her personal definition of success, which she measures by the standards and goals she sets for herself for "today and tomorrow":

> "... [A]nd it's my own sense of accomplishment, my own internal measure, that I think gives me the measure of achievement. If I think I've accomplished what I set out to accomplish, then that's achievement."

She has also used her capacity as a role model to encourage youth, both girls and boys, with an emphasis on girls, to have a positive influence on the planet. When asked in a 2004 interview about the world's biggest problem, she replied, "the global environment and how we are having an impact on the global environment." Using her "perspective from space" to give her argument added impact, she said,

"[Earth is] the only planet we've got, and you can see the effect of humanity when you look back at Earth from space. You can see it in a lot of different areas. You can see smog over the cities, you can see pollution in the water. Our satellites can measure differences in the atmosphere, and it's starting to accumulate to a point that we may not be able to correct the problem if we don't do something about it pretty soon."

Sally sends a strong message to youth: "You can make a difference."

As an astronaut, Sally was already exhibiting the qualities of leadership and cooperation that she would put to use in her teaching and in Sally Ride Science. Sally was a recipient of the Von Braun Award, which is given to people who have the attitude, leadership qualities, and ability to inspire others in promoting "a visionary outlook toward space flight."

Sally has also been inducted into the Astronaut Hall of Fame as the First American Female in Space. She's in the National Women's Hall of Fame and the California Hall of Fame as well. In 1988, Sally received the National Collegiate Athletic Association (NCAA) Theodore Roosevelt Award for lifetime achievement by an individual who has shown excellent athletic abilities in college.

Sally's mission to cultivate and encourage the natural curiosity in youth has not gone unnoticed. She has been awarded numerous medals recognizing her positive influence on society, including the Jefferson Award for Public Service, an award that recognizes "individuals for their achievements and contributions through public and community service." Another great honor was the naming of two elementary schools after her: Sally K. Ride Elementary School in The Woodlands, Texas, and Sally K. Ride Elementary School in Germantown, Maryland.

> *"I would like to be remembered as someone who was not afraid to do what she wanted to do, and as someone who took risks along the way in order to achieve her goals."*
>
> Sally Ride

Considering that Sally's life mission after leaving NASA has been to increase people's quality of life through science, it is not surprising that she has had such a lasting impact on the world. Her idea for EarthKAM, the project that puts students in charge of a camera in space, has involved almost 1,000 middle schools from across the United States and engaged tens of thousands more school children in real science. Sally Ride Science has been nurturing the love of science in girls for over a decade and, every year, there are more programs added. In the first five years alone, over 30,000 young girls were involved, not including the students who have used classroom materials created by her.

As Sally saw the way the education system seemed directed toward boys and not girls, she saw how her accomplishments could be used to influence a new generation. "Everywhere I go, I run into girls who've been to space camp and want to be astronauts. Or they love animals and want to become zoologists," Sally said. "I would love to see those same stars in their eyes in ten or fifteen years and know they're on their way."

SALLY RIDE, HERO

Perhaps Sally's legacy lies most obviously in the impressions she has made on thousands of individual young girls, like Sofia, who lives somewhere in the United States and posted the following on the Internet:

> *"Sally Ride is important to me because she encouraged women to love science. She showed that women can do whatever men can do. She made a difference in my life since I'm a girl and women can do just as much as boys and men do. Also, Sally Ride is a great role model for people who have big dreams. I'm glad women like Sally Ride encourage girls like me to be whatever we want to. She is my hero!"*

Sally Ride in 2003 before the insignia of the STS–107 mission.

Chronology

1951 Sally Kristen Ride is born in Encino, California.

1957 The Soviet Union launches the first artificial object into Earth's orbit, the satellite *Sputnik I.*

1958 President Dwight D. Eisenhower creates the National Aeronautics and Space Administration, or NASA.

1961 Sally's family goes to Europe, where Sally learns to play tennis. Soviet cosmonaut Yuri Gagarin becomes the first human in space.

1962 Sally wins a scholarship to Westlake Private School for girls.

1963 The Soviet Union sends the first woman into space, Valentina Tereshkova.

1966 Sally enters Swarthmore College in Pennsylvania but quits after three months to concentrate on tennis.

1968 Sally enrolls at Stanford University and takes a double major in physics and English literature.

1969 NASA sends the first humans to the Moon. Neil Armstrong and Buzz Aldrin walk on the lunar surface while Michael Collins orbits above in the command module.

1971 Sally Ride completes her Bachelor of Science degree.

1973 Sally Ride begins work on a doctoral degree in physics.

1977 In her final year in school, Sally sees a NASA advertisement for astronaut openings in the space program. She applies and is accepted to become an astronaut in training.

1981 NASA's space shuttle is flown into space for the first time.

1982 Sally Ride marries fellow astronaut Steve Hawley.

1983 Sally makes her first flight in the space shuttle *Challenger* with Mission STS–7, becoming the first American woman in space.

1984 Sally makes a second trip into space on the *Challenger* with Mission STS–41G.

1986 The space shuttle *Challenger* disintegrates after liftoff, killing all seven crew members, including schoolteacher Christa McAuliffe. Sally is a spectator and later is part of the team that investigates the cause of the tragedy. The accident dramatically changes her career.

1987 Sally spends a year as NASA's advisor on future plans to explore space. She then quits NASA and returns to the university and the study of science. Sally and Steve divorce.

1987–1988 Sally is a science fellow at the Center for International Security and Arms Control (CISAC) at Stanford University, where she studies the banning of nuclear weapons.

1989 The space shuttle program begins again. Sally accepts a position as director and professor of physics at the University of California, San Diego.

1995 KidSat, a joint project between NASA and Sally Ride, puts children in control of a camera mounted in the space shuttle. The program is renamed EarthKAM in 1997.

1998 The first section of the International Space Station (ISS) is placed in orbit.

1999 Sally Ride becomes president of the company Space.com. Eileen Collins is NASA's first female flight commander, for space shuttle Mission STS–93. Sally watches the launch of Eileen's mission.

2001 Sally quits her job as president of Space.com. She forms the company Sally Ride Science to help generate interest in science among children, especially girls.

2003 The space shuttle *Columbia* disintegrates upon re-entry into Earth's atmosphere. Its seven crew members perish. Sally is assigned to the disaster investigation committee.

2010 For the first time, four women are in space at one time, aboard the space shuttle and the ISS. The space shuttle program retires at the end of the year.

Glossary

aeronautics The science and practice of moving through air

Apollo program NASA's program to send humans to the Moon

arc A curve

arms race A competition between countries to accumulate more weapons than the other

astronaut A person trained to pilot, navigate, and participate as a crew member aboard a spacecraft

astrophysics The branch of astronomy (the study of space) that looks at the physical and chemical processes that occur in stars, galaxies, and the rest of space

atom The basic unit of an element. The size of the atom is distinct to each element, or kind of matter, while the materials that make up the atom are common to all matter.

civilian A passenger aboard a spacecraft who is not an employee of a space agency such as NASA

Cold War A continuing state of tension and hostility between two or more countries without physical combat but characterized by threats, spying, and arms build-up. The best-known modern example of this was the Cold War between the United States and the Soviet Union from after World War II to the early 1990s.

coolant A gas or liquid used to lower the temperature of a piece of equipment

commercial Done with the purpose of generating money

disarming Reducing or limiting the number of weapons owned by a country

fiber optic Used to describe something made of thin glass strands, or fibers, and often used to transmit information

foreign affairs The activities of one nation in relation to other nations

galaxy A cluster of star systems, containing on average 100 billion stars and separated from other galaxies by large areas of empty space. The galaxy in which our star, the Sun, is located is called the Milky Way.

GPS or global positioning system A network of satellites that determine the location of the user and communicate that information to the user's receiver, which is usually a small device that is handheld or installed in a vehicle

gravity The physical force one object exerts on another through attraction; the bigger the object, the greater the force. The closer an object is to another, the greater the force. Earth's gravity keeps the Moon in its orbit. The Moon's gravity causes the ocean tides.

ground control The staff members on the ground who monitor and aid the progress of spacecraft

interstellar The space not occupied by large bodies such as stars and planets and occupied by microscopic pieces of matter

legacy What someone leaves behind; a gift or contribution to society

O-ring A piece of rubber compressed in a joint to create a seal

operational The status of a vehicle or piece of equipment after it has been tested to ensure it works as designed

orbit The circular path taken by an object as it travels around another object

protocol A standard plan of action

microchip A thin piece of material with miniature electronic circuits. This technology is used today in all electronic equipment.

molecule The smallest particle of a substance that has all the properties of that substance

nuclear warhead The explosive device in a nuclear weapon; the part that contains both the nuclear material and the explosive that sets off the nuclear explosion

rocket An engine that is forced upward by the burning of gas or liquid fuel in a chamber at the bottom of a tube

shock wave A disturbance or reaction resulting in waves of energy in a medium such as air or water

simulate To create an imitation that mimics reality

space walk An activity in which an astronaut purposefully leaves a spacecraft when in space, in a space suit, to perform repairs and other tasks

Soviet Union A former nation made up of a group of communist republics in parts of eastern Europe and northern Asia. The Soviet Union dissolved in 1991, creating a group of independent, non-communist nations out of its former republics, including Russia, Ukraine, Kazakhstan, and Georgia.

T minus zero A term referring to the exact moment of liftoff in a launch. One minute before liftoff would be "T minus one minute." The time *after* liftoff is given as "T plus one second . . . T plus one minute," and so on.

Further Information

Books

Gueldenpfennig, Sonia. *Spectacular Women in Space.*
Toronto, ON: Second Story Press, 2004.

Macidull, John C. *Challenger's Shadow: Did Government and Industry Management Kill Seven Astronauts?* Tamarac, FL: Llumina Press, 2002.

Nichols, Catherine. *Sally Ride.* Danbury, CT: Children's Press, 2005.

Nolen, Stephanie. *Promised the Moon: The Untold Story of the First Women in the Space Race.* Toronto, ON: Penguin Canada, 2002.

Ride, Sally, and Susan Okie. *To Space & Back.*
Toronto, ON: HarperCollins, 1989.

Wearing, Judy. *Roberta Bondar: Canada's First Woman in Space.*
New York, NY and St. Catharines, ON: Crabtree Publishing, 2011.

Web sites

www.sallyridescience.com
Find information on the Sally Ride Science festivals, the Toy Challenge design contest, and Sally's other projects for kids interested in getting involved in science.

www.space.com
Get up-to-the minute news on current space news and research. Watch live streaming video of shuttle and rocket launches, and look at thousands of spectacular photographs of space.

www.srl.caltech.edu/ACE
Follow the Advanced Composition Explorer (ACE), a solar system probe launched in 1997. The ongoing project has the probe positioned 900,000 miles (1.5 million km) away from Earth and measures the solar wind, interplanetary magnetic field, and higher energy particles accelerated by the Sun, as well as particles accelerated in the galactic regions beyond.

https://earthkam.ucsd.edu
Sign up to take part in missions or browse the pictures and projects other school kids have been working on with the help of Sally Ride's EarthKAM project.

www.nytimes.com/2003/08/26/science/space/26CONV.html
In this interview with the *New York Times* in 2003, Sally Ride answers questions about the Columbia disaster, why it happened, the role NASA played in the accident, and what is next in her own life.

http://news.bbc.co.uk/2/hi/technology/8407139.stm
Read what Sally Ride tells the British Broadcasting Corporation (BBC) in 2009 about the importance of science and technology to young people and what needs to be done about it.

www.jsc.nasa.gov/Bios/htmlbios/ride-sk.html
Sally Ride's official NASA biography and photograph.

www.sallyridescience.com/festivals/video/wmv
Watch the video to get an idea of what it is like to attend a Sally Ride Science festival.

www.youtube.com/watch?v=C8Eb5voc1Sw
Hear what Sally has to say about being selected as America's first female astronaut.

Index

Index

About the Author

Tom Riddolls never quite figured out what he wanted to be when he grew up. When asked at the age of six, he replied, "I want to be a bird." Obviously that never happened and, since that time, Tom has done many things to keep busy: cleaning ancient stone statues in Africa, writing articles for magazines and books for children, and currently working in a university laboratory teaching students about the science of materials.